The Introd
Flying Le

The Introductory
Flying Lesson

Jeremy M Pratt

Published by

www.afeonline.com

First Edition 1996
Revised Edition 1999

Second Edition 2001

Third Edition 2002
Revised Edition 2003
Fourth Edition 2006

Revised Fourth Edition 2009

The Introductory Flying Lesson

ISBN 978 1 906559 120

Printed in Malta by Melita Press

www.afeonline.com

Airplan Flight Equipment Ltd
1a Ringway Trading Estate, Shadowmoss Road, Manchester M22 5LH
Tel: 0161 499 0023   Fax: 0161 499 0298
email: enquiries@afeonline.com
www.afeonline.com

Contents

What is an Introductory Flying Lesson?

What is an Introductory Flying Lesson?

The introductory lesson is Exercise 3 of the training course for a Private Pilot's Licence (PPL). In case you're wondering, Exercises 1 & 2 consist of ground instruction about the aircraft itself and procedures before and after flight. Exercise 3 is also commonly known the 'trial lesson', or 'air experience'. Whatever the flying school chooses to call this flight, the objective is the same. It is the chance to fly in a light aircraft or microlight and to try your hand at actually piloting it under the supervision of a flying instructor.

That is what an introductory lesson is. There are a couple of things that it definitely is not. An introductory lesson is not the same as a pleasure flight, where you might sit in the back of the aircraft and the pilot is, in effect, an aerial chauffeur. The introductory lesson is a flight where you get to do some actual piloting, it is an introduction to the art of flying an aircraft. That said, the introductory lesson is not an irrevocable commitment to learn to fly. Plenty of people take an introductory lesson just for the experience, as you might try sailing a boat or driving a racing car just the once. There is nothing wrong with that at all – even though some pilots find it difficult to believe that anyone wouldn't want to learn to fly! Beware though, flying can be addictive. There are plenty of pilots who got started by deciding to have an introductory lesson just for the fun of it, and found themselves hooked!

Many flying schools offer introductory lessons of differing durations, 30 or 60 minutes are typical options. Some flying schools may offer a 'land away' option, flying to another airfield and landing there before returning to base, so that you can appreciate the touring capabilities of a light aircraft. The distance such a flight can cover is limited to avoid contravening Civil Aviation Authority (CAA) air charter rules, but it does give you the chance to experience two take-offs and landings, and a surprising amount of what you learn on the first flight can be put into practice in the second. The introductory lesson voucher (if there is one) may state the duration of the lesson, and the flying school staff will be pleased to confirm this for you. A flight officially starts from the moment the aircraft starts to 'taxy' away from the parking spot, and it officially ends when the aircraft parks after landing. Clearly, the 'official' flying time is longer than the actual time airborne, but the duration of the official flight is the basis of the time that pilots record in their flying logbooks and so it is normally this 'chocks to chocks' time that the flying school charges.

If you are thinking of learning to fly, it is worth knowing that the flying time on this flight *does* count towards the total required for completing the PPL course, of which more later. If you buy a logbook at the time of the introductory lesson your instructor will help you enter the details of your flight, and you will have logged your first flight time on the way to becoming a pilot.

A pilot's logbook

The Flying
Instructor,
The Aircraft,
The Flying School

The Flying Instructor,
The Aircraft,
The Flying School

Your introductory lesson must be flown with a fully licensed Flight Instructor. Unlike learning to drive, for instance, you cannot learn to fly with any pilot – the person teaching you must have an instructor qualification. Even a senior airline captain or ace fighter pilot cannot teach you to fly if he or she is not a licensed Flight Instructor (sometimes also called a flying instructor), not even on an introductory lesson.

To become a flying instructor, a pilot first has to build up a minimum number of flying hours and obtain certain ratings. Then he or she has to undertake an intensive flight instructor course and pass a flying test at the end. To remain qualified, instructors have to comply with currency and renewal requirements. As a matter of interest, many flight instructors are also licensed commercial or airline pilots.

The instructor sits in the right-hand seat

This much flight instructors have in common. Aside from these qualifications, flying instructors, like any other cross-section of people, come in all shapes and sizes. Your flight instructor may be a dedicated full-time instructor, a full-time airline pilot or military pilot who also instructs, or possibly a part-time instructor who flies at weekends only. What all flying instructors share is a real commitment to flying. It requires a certain amount of dedication (and usually their own hard-earned cash) to become an instructor – not every pilot has the ability, or the desire, to achieve an instructor rating. Instructors are almost invariably keen to pass on their knowledge and enthusiasm for flying and they are, after all, there to help you learn.

Piper PA-28 Warrior

Cessna 172

Robin

Aerospatiale Tampico

Cessna C152

Diamond DA40

The aircraft in which you will be flying will be some type of single engine training aircraft. Common types include American Piper or Cessna aircraft; French Robin or Aerospatiale types; British Slingsby or Austrian/Canadian Diamond aircraft. If your lesson is to be in a 'three-axis' microlight aircraft, common types include the Eurostar, the Ikarus and the Rans. The 'three-axis' microlight is, to all intents and purposes a small aeroplane, though it has a lower weight limit than a single engine aircraft and generally has less comprehensive radios and equipment.

EV-97 Eurostar

Ikarus C42

Rans Coyote

Not all aircraft types are approved to be used for flying training, including for example most home-built or kit-built designs and ex-military aircraft. The training aircraft you fly in will have full dual flying controls and indeed virtually all aircraft with more than one seat are equipped with dual controls. These flying controls are explained in more detail later. To be used for flying instruction, a training aircraft must be maintained to a more rigorous schedule than an aircraft utilised solely for private use. It may be maintained by licensed engineers at an approved organisation, and it has to be inspected and serviced at regular intervals. On the side of the aircraft will be its registration letters, for example G-ABCD. Pilots tend to identify individual aircraft of a fleet by the last two letters of its registration, using the phonetic alphabet. So G-ABCD would be known as "Golf – Alpha Bravo Charlie Delta" – or just "Charlie Delta". This is also the identification often used as the radio callsign too.

A training aircraft is, as you would expect, relatively docile and easy to fly. Nevertheless, it will almost certainly cruise comfortably at more than 100mph, and be capable of flying for several hours before needing to refuel. Because aircraft fly (mostly) in straight lines, even a relatively slow aircraft can fly some way in a short space of time – you may be surprised at the distance covered during just a brief local flight. Although the aircraft will be capable of climbing well above 10,000 feet (around 3,000m), it is not common to climb this high during a training flight, and you can expect to fly not much higher than 3000 feet (around 1,000 metres) or so.

On first acquaintance a light aircraft or three-axis microlight can seem a bit, well, frail – especially if your previous experience of aircraft has been limited to airliners! Happily, appearances are deceptive in this case. Even a small aeroplane is very strong, and it is built and maintained to a much higher standard than a car. It may well be certified to speeds of nearly 200mph, altitudes well in excess of 10,000 feet and flight loads of 4-6G. Even at these limits, the aircraft structure has plenty of strength in reserve, and during a normal flight it will not come anywhere near it's certified limits. It is quite possible that the aircraft you will be flying in is used for regular flights of several hundred miles or more, and it may have been flown across the Atlantic or across Europe when it was first delivered from the factory. The aircraft will also have many duplicated systems – duplicate flying controls, two fuel tanks, two ignition systems, back-up electrical power etc.

The flying school provides the facilities for proper flying instruction, and may offer a very wide range of flying courses including training for commercial licences and ratings. Those responsible for the smooth running of the school are often referred to as the 'ground staff' or 'operations', and these unsung heroes will normally be your first point of contact at the flying school. These people have a lot to do in a busy flying school – everything from answering the phone and organising the flying schedule to ensuring that the aircraft are refuelled, and even making the coffee. Many operations staff in flying schools are aspiring professional pilots themselves.

In charge of flying standards and the flying staff there will be a Chief Flying Instructor – CFI. This person will be an experienced instructor and probably an examiner too, and in matters concerning flying at the school the CFI usually has the final word.

Before You Arrive at the Flying School

Before You Arrive at the Flying School

With your lesson booked and confirmed with the flying school, you only have to wait for the big day to come round.

The first point to remember on the day itself is that flying training, and particularly a first lesson, is very reliant on reasonable weather conditions. It is always advisable to call the flying school before you set-out to check that the weather is suitable – this call could save a wasted journey. Even if the sun is shining and there is not a cloud in the sky, fog at the airfield or thick haze may force a cancellation, so do check ahead. Safety, first and foremost, is the criteria that will decide if the weather is suitable for flying, and no self-respecting flying instructor will take you flying if he or she thinks the weather will make it difficult for you to learn anything useful. If the flying school does have to cancel your lesson you can do no more than be patient, and book another date. Conversely, even if the weather looks dreadful where you are, it is still worth checking with the flying school. The weather may be better at the airfield, or they may offer you the opportunity to be shown around the school and its aircraft, postponing the actual flight to another day.

Your lesson will only take place if weather conditions are suitable

Call your school on the day to confirm
that your lesson is still on...

In a modern training aeroplane there is no need for any special clothing, whatever you wear on the way to the airfield should be suitable to wear in the aircraft. The only particular point is that high heels are not ideal for flying, just as they are not for driving a car. The flying suits, goggles and helmets much beloved of countless flying movies will be nowhere to be seen, and you are highly unlikely to wear a parachute as most light aircraft (with the exception of some vintage and aerobatic types) are not equipped with them. Neither will you need to wear an oxygen mask as extra oxygen does not become necessary until you are above 10–12,000 feet.

All-in-all, the general advice is 'come as you are', although there is one thing which may need to be considered more closely, namely alcohol. The consumption of even a modest amount of alcohol is highly inadvisable before a flying lesson and the legal alcohol limit for pilots is far stricter than for drivers. Additionally, with increasing altitude the effect of alcohol is magnified several times over. All airlines refuse boarding to drunk passengers because of the danger they can pose to the aircraft's crew and passengers, and in a small aircraft the potential consequences are no less serious. Most flying schools will refuse to allow anybody who has been drinking into one of their aircraft. Safety is, after all, the first and foremost consideration in flying and even aside from the security issue, you are highly unlikely to get much enjoyment from a flight under these circumstances. Likewise, flying with a hangover is not to be recommended.

If on the day of your introductory lesson you are not feeling well for any reason don't hesitate to ring the flying school and cancel the lesson – you can always fly another day. It is also inadvisable to fly if you have a cold or if your ears are blocked in some way. If you do have to cancel your lesson for whatever reason, all flying schools will appreciate the maximum notice you can give so that they have the best chance of releasing the aircraft for somebody else. To operate efficiently the flying school has to make good utilisation of its aircraft, and an aircraft sitting on the ground waiting for somebody who doesn't appear is a very expensive and frustrating proposition for a flying school. It's also hard on instructors, who tend to be paid by the flying hour.

On a brighter note, if you have been given an introductory lesson voucher, don't forget to take it with you. And if you have a video or camera you can take that along as well. Even the least photogenic flying instructor will normally be happy to pose with you beside the aircraft you fly in!

Typical views from a light aircraft

Before Getting to the Aircraft

Before Getting to the Aircraft

Once you arrive at the flying school you should go to the reception and the ground staff will tell you if there are any delays or changes. Flying schools all try their best to keep to schedule, but they are susceptible to weather problems or operational delays that can disrupt an otherwise well-organised flying programme.

At this stage you may well be asked to fill-out a simple membership form that makes you a temporary member of the flying school. This is a standard procedure and is something that the school's insurance company probably insist on. It is a sad fact of life that even in a single flying lesson such mundane legal matters may intrude.

You will probably now meet your instructor. He or she may ask if you live locally, so that the flight can be routed over your house if possible. Your instructor will also give you an overview of the weather situation and the expected format for the flight. You should receive some form of pre-flight briefing – essentially an informal chat to give you an idea of how to fly the aircraft and what will be covered in this lesson. Many instructors will be interested to know how seriously you are thinking of taking-up flying. They can then format the flight accordingly so that you can get the best out of it. At this stage, and throughout the flight, you should feel free to ask any questions you have, or query anything that you do not fully understand. The instructor is there to help you and there's no such thing as a stupid question, only a stupid answer! Like many other professions, flying has a wide range of vocabulary and 'buzz-words' all of its own. Many people in the flying business use these words and expressions without even realising it, so don't hesitate to ask for a 'plain language' explanation of anything incomprehensible. If you are interested, there is a glossary and list of abbreviations at the back of this book.

Before leaving the flying school building the instructor will complete the necessary paperwork and may need to telephone an Air Traffic unit on the airfield to give advance details of the flight. Then it's time to walk-out to the aircraft, and at many airfields you may be required to wear a 'high visibility' vest whilst around the aircraft parking area – if this is the case the flying school will provide one for you.

At the aircraft the instructor will probably first get you seated in the cockpit. Getting in (and out) of the cockpit can be a lesson in itself. If the aircraft has a low-wing you will probably step up onto the wing before entering the cockpit, the instructor will point-out the designated 'walkway' that you can stand on, and ask you not to step off it. You may see small notices marked "No Step" or similar, it goes without saying that you should keep off these! Entry to the cockpit itself may be via a door, or alternatively the top part of the cockpit may slide back or hinge up so that you can step into the aircraft. Entry into a high wing aircraft may be simpler, although you should be aware of the need to stoop down under the wing.

Do not walk or step on any part of the aircraft marked with 'No Step' placards or red warning signs as on this Eurostar

Either way, your instructor will show you how to get into the aircraft and help you get settled into your seat. You will notice that you are sitting on the left-hand side of the aircraft, with most of the instruments and switches directly in front of you. In essence the left-side seat is where the captain (or Pilot In Command, it's the same thing) sits. As a trainee pilot you occupy this seat because you are training to one day fly as Pilot In Command.

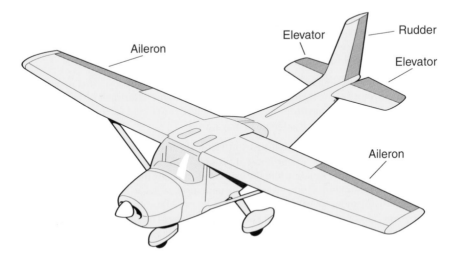

The control column controls the elevator and ailerons, the rudder pedals control the rudder

The 'control sticks' of a Eurostar

Directly in front of you will be the main flying controls – the control column and the rudder pedals. The control column can take two forms: it may be a stick which comes up from the cockpit floor, or a control wheel – rather like a sawn-off steering wheel – mounted on the end

of a pole in the instrument panel. Either design is
normally referred to as the 'control column' and
both types work in the same way. Pushing the
control column forward and back controls the
aircraft in pitch, making the nose of the aircraft
pitch up (when pulled back) or pitch down (when
pushed forward) as seen from the cockpit. Moving
the stick from side to side (or rotating the control
wheel) controls the aircraft in roll. To bank the
aircraft to the left the control column is moved (or
rotated) to the left, and vice versa.

A control 'wheel' in a Cessna 152

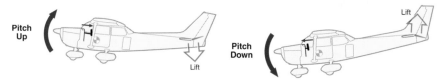

Moving the control column back makes the aircraft pitch up, moving the control column forward
makes the aircraft pitch down

Moving the control column to the left makes the aircraft roll to the left, moving the control column
to the right makes the aircraft roll to the right

The rudder pedals are on the floor under the
control panel, there will be a left and a right
pedal, one for each foot. The rudder pedals
control the aircraft in yaw – making the nose of
the aircraft move from side to side as seen from
the cockpit. Pressing the left pedal moves the nose
to the left, and vice versa.

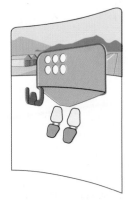

Rudder Pedals

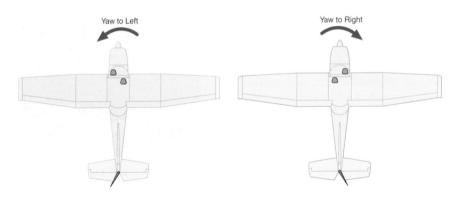

Pressing the left rudder pedal yaws the aircraft to the left, pressing on the right rudder pedal yaws the aircraft to the right

Once in your seat the instructor will show you how to adjust the seat (where possible). The most important factor is that you should be able to reach the flying controls easily, without having to stretch out, and you should also be able to see over the instrument panel and out over the nose of the aircraft. Once airborne you will control the aircraft by reference to the view ahead, so it is worth spending a few moments now to make sure that the seat is adjusted to give you the best view ahead and a good reach on the flying controls. Some aircraft and three-axis microlights may use extra cushions to help you find a comfortable seating position.

At this stage, the instructor may leave the cockpit to walk around the aircraft carrying out the pre-flight checks (alternatively these may have been done before taking you out to the aircraft). The pre-flight check is an established ritual in flying, and it applies just as much to a Boeing 747 about to make a trans-continental flight, as to a microlight about to fly once

around the airfield. The instructor will make a tour around the aircraft, prodding, shaking, peering and examining various bits and pieces to satisfy him/herself that it is fit to fly. Even if the aircraft has only just come back from a flight, the pilot about to take it should always perform this check. Don't be alarmed if you see the instructor muttering or mumbling to him/herself during the pre-flight check. Many pilots do this (most without realising it), they're narrating the things they are checking, as if reciting a poem learnt off by heart!

A pilot making a 'pre-flight' check of Cessna 152

The very simple instrument panel of a 3-axis Microlight...

...and the flat screen 'glass cockpit' displays of a Piper Warrior. Don't worry too much about the instruments – you'll mostly be looking out of the window.

You may have a spare minute to look at the instrument panel in front of you. Do not be put off if it seems to be filled with incomprehensible dials, indicators and instruments. You will only need to refer to a few of these during the flight, and in fact you will control the aircraft almost solely by reference to the view outside. The six principle flight instruments, not all of which may be fitted to the aircraft you fly, are:

The **Attitude Indicator,** which shows a miniature picture of the aircraft's attitude in relation to the horizon (e.g. nose up, nose down, banked etc.), it is sometimes still referred to as the Artificial Horizon.

The **Heading Indicator,** which indicates the aircraft's heading in degrees of the compass (also sometimes known as the Direction Indicator – DI).

The **Altimeter,** which shows height of the aircraft in hundreds of feet above a fixed datum, the usual reference is sea level.

The **Airspeed Indicator,** which measures the airflow and displays this in terms of speed through the air.

The **Vertical Speed Indicator** which shows the rate at which the aircraft is climbing or descending in hundreds of feet per minute.

The **Turn Indicator** which shows the rate at which the aircraft is turning, and whether or not the aircraft is in balance.

The aircraft may be fitted with electronic flight displays – a so-called 'glass cockpit'. Although the presentation is different, the principles are the same for both types of flight instrument display.

An AirSpeed Indicator – ASI

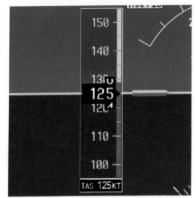

A 'speed tape' on an electronic cockpit display

The Airspeed Indicator, the Heading Indicator and the Altimeter are probably of most interest during the introductory lesson, and so are worth looking at a little more closely.

The **Airspeed Indicator** measures the pressure of the airflow from a sensing point known as the pitot, this is usually found under the wing. The pressure sensed is converted by the instrument into a measurement of speed, and displayed by a needle which moves around the dial or a 'speed tape' on an electronic display. The speed scale will commonly be calibrated in miles per hour (mph), or knots. A knot is a speed of one nautical mile per hour and a nautical mile is slightly longer than the statute mile measured on a car speedometer, so for example 90 knots is equivalent to about 100mph. Knots are commonly used for flying speeds, and wind speed is also mostly given in knots. The airspeed is a very important factor in controlling an aircraft, and you will find that a pilot pays particular attention to the Airspeed Indicator during the take-off and initial climb, and during the approach and landing.

The **Heading Indicator** is driven by a gyroscope, and is set by reference to a compass. When correctly set, the Heading Indicator will show the direction in which the aircraft is heading. The dial is divided into degrees around the points of the compass, where north is 360°, east is 90°, south is 180° and west is 270°. The Heading Indicator is normally marked around the edge with lines every 10°, and a shorter line for intermediate 5°. Some simpler aircraft and three-axis microlights may use a compass instead of a heading indicator.

A Heading Indicator

The **Altimeter** senses the air pressure outside the aircraft and converts this into an indication of altitude, on the basis that pressure decreases with height. An electronic display will have an altitude 'tape'. The dial of a 'round dial' altimeter will have two main pointers: a long pointer which indicates hundreds of feet, and a shorter one that indicates thousands of feet. The Altimeter will also have a small 'window' in which a set of numbers is visible, this is called the 'sub-scale'. Because pressure changes every day as weather systems move across the globe, the altimeter has to be reset frequently in order for it to give an accurate reading. Before take-off, the instructor will obtain a pressure setting called 'QNH', and set this number on the altimeter sub-scale. When QNH is set, the altimeter will indicate the aircraft's altitude above sea level, for example on the ground at the airfield it should display the airfield's elevation – its altitude above sea level. When returning to the airfield to land, the altimeter setting may be changed to the QFE setting. When QFE is set, the altimeter will indicate the aircraft's height above the airfield.

An Altimeter

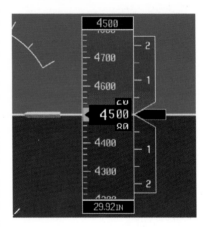

An 'altitude tape' on an electronic cockpit display

Once the instructor is seated in the aircraft beside you, you will be shown how to fasten and adjust the seat belt/harness. There is no need for this to be breathtakingly tight; a snug, comfortable fit is just right. The instructor will also show you how to release the seat belt/harness, how to open the door or canopy, and point-out any particular safety features. This is the equivalent of the safety briefing you will have seen as a passenger in an airliner and just like airline cabin crew, your instructor will appreciate it if you pay attention!

The instructor will now run through the pre-starting checks, probably with the aid of a checklist. The pre-starting checks will include moving the flight controls, and you will be able to see the elevator and ailerons responding to the movement of the control column. Items such as the instruments and ancillary controls will also be checked now, in preparation for starting the engine.

A typical aviation headset

Once the engine is running you will probably put on a headset. The headset is simply a set of headphones that go over the ears, with a microphone mounted on a boom that is positioned in front of the mouth. The instructor will show you how to adjust the headband so that the ear cups fit snugly on your head. There is no need to tighten the headband so that your head is gripped like being in a vice, but you do want the headset secure enough not to slip off. Move the headband so that it sits right on the crown of your head for best comfort. The microphone is positioned by moving the boom so that the microphone is just in front of your lips, say about 4cm away. There may well be a volume control on the ear cup, so that you can adjust the volume to suit.

Once you are wearing the headset, with the radio on, you should be able to hear the conversation between aircraft and ATC on the radio, and also the voice of your instructor (and your own voice) via the intercom which links the headsets within the aircraft. There is no need to press any button to speak on the intercom, the microphone will be permanently 'live', or voice activated, to work over the intercom. With the headset on and properly adjusted you should be able to carry on a conversation with the instructor at normal speaking levels. To transmit a message over the radio, the instructor will press a transmit button (sometimes labelled PTT – Press To Transmit), which is often mounted on the control column. Unlike a telephone conversation, radio communication is a 'one-way' process, only one person can talk at a time. You may see the instructor listening out and waiting for a gap in radio transmissions before pressing the PTT button to transmit a message.

Although the intercom does make conversation within the aircraft very easy, the background chatter of the radio can be a bit of distraction. Most experienced pilots have the knack of being constantly aware of what is being said on the radio, turning their full attention to it when a message relevant to their aircraft is broadcast; so occasionally the instructor may have to interrupt a conversation with you to listen to something on the radio or to acknowledge a message. Don't worry if the radio messages sound like a steam of verbal nonsense. Most people find the radio like that at first, but it soon becomes quite comprehensible when you know some of the standard conventions and vocabulary.

The instructor will look after setting the radio frequencies: at a small airfield there may be just one radio frequency in use, whilst a larger airfield may have several frequencies, each providing a different service.

When the aircraft is ready to move off the instructor will release the parking brake, increase the power and taxy the aircraft towards the runway. Steering on the ground is accomplished through the rudder pedals, and in most aircraft types these have a direct connection to the nose wheel (the vast majority of training aircraft have a nose wheel as opposed to tail wheel), which steers to the left and right. There may also be a set of toe brakes, activated by pressing the top half of each rudder pedal, or separate plates above the rudder pedals. Toe brakes operate the wheel brakes on the main undercarriage and can be used differentially, so that just the right or just the left brake is applied, turning the aircraft in that direction. Some aircraft have just nose wheel steering, some have just differential braking (with a freely castoring nose wheel), and some have both.

The instructor will usually taxy to a place on the airfield known as the 'holding point', a spot close to the active runway. Here the instructor will stop the aircraft and carry out the power and pre take-off checks. What? More checks! You will soon realise that a light aircraft is operated to the same standards of professionalism as a large airliner. The basic philosophy is to check rather than assume, check again just to be sure, and to take nothing for granted in the meantime!

The power checks consist of increasing the engine power to near cruise setting and then verifying that the engine systems are functioning properly and that the instrument indications are all normal. The pre take-off checks that follow ensure that the aircraft is ready to fly, and are a final re-check that vital systems (such as the flying controls) are working properly and are set-up as they should be.

For these checks the instructor will probably have lined-up the aircraft to face into wind. Landing and take-off will always be done as closely as possible into the wind, this applies just as much to the biggest airliner as to a small training aircraft. Taking-off and landing into wind reduces the length of runway used and gives the aircraft a better climb angle after take-off. You may see the instructor look at the windsock to check the wind, and the wind speed and direction may also be passed over the radio, for example, "Surface wind 240 degrees, 10 knots".

With the checks complete, and usually with a final inquiry to yourself to make sure that you are ready to fly, the instructor may radio for permission to take-off (this is not always necessary at a small airfield). Then, with a final look around to make sure that the runway and approach is clear, you will taxy onto the runway and turn towards the direction of take-off. The runway is ahead of you, the sky lies beyond: the time to fly has come.

You may well see your instructor referring to the aircraft's checklist

How Aircraft Fly

How Aircraft Fly

Most people who have more than a passing interest in aircraft will wonder from time to time what forces are at work to make the whole business of flying possible. Even a qualified pilot, watching several hundred tonnes of airliner lifting gracefully into the sky with little apparent effort, is sometimes prone to think the same way!

Before going any further it ought to be stated here that a knowledge of the basic principles of flight, as instructors like to call the process that keeps aircraft airborne, is not at all essential at this stage. After all, birds fly perfectly well without ever having been instructed in the mysteries of lift, drag etc. and the early pioneer pilots flew aircraft before many of the principles of flight were fully understood. If you are happy to accept that aircraft fly because they are meant to (and there's plenty of evidence to show that this is true), then there is no reason not read through this section. On the other hand, if you would like to know a little more about the processes involved, read on.

The principle force at work which allows an aircraft to take-off and fly, rather than just ploughing off the end of the runway as a surface vehicle would, is *lift*.

Lift is generated by the aircraft's wings, and in normal level flight the wings are generating an amount of lift equal to the weight of the aircraft. Thus, in level flight if a light aircraft weighs 700kg (1540lbs), the wings are generating 700kg of lift to keep the aircraft flying at a constant level.

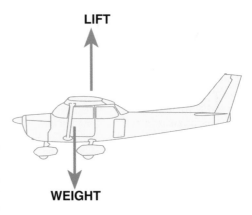

Lift opposes weight

If you look at a cross-section through a wing, you will notice a fairly distinctive 'airfoil' shape. As the airflow reaches the wing, a combination of this shape, the airflow speed, and the angle at which the airflow meets the wing, causes a difference in the speed of the airflow above and below the wing. The airflow over the wing's top surface is faster than the airflow beneath it. It is a basic property of moving air that a faster airflow speed is associated with reduced pressure. So, the airflow speed and the angle at which it meets the wing creates a pressure differential – the pressure above the wing is less than the pressure below it. That force acts from high pressure towards low pressure and in this instance is called lift.

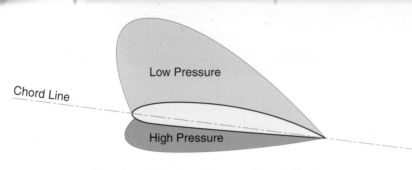

Generation of lift by the airflow around the airfoil section

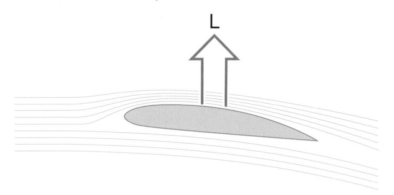

There are plenty of examples of lift outside the aviation world, for example the 'wings' on racing cars that provide lift in a downwards direction – downforce – to keep the cars pressed down onto the road at high speeds. The lift (downforce) generated by even these small surfaces can be several times greater than the weight of the car itself. So, in theory, a racing car could drive along the roof of a tunnel, the downforce keeping it pressed onto the surface. The only problem is, if the car slows down it will generate less lift, and eventually it will fall off – maybe this is why nobody had tried this out for real! Hydrofoils on high-speed boats are also wings, operating in water instead of air to lift the boat hull clear of the water at high speed.

If you are intrigued enough to try a small experiment, take a flat piece of card or thick paper and crease or bend it slightly across the middle. If you now hold this peice of card or paper close to your lips and blow across the top of it, the card or paper will lift up into the airflow you are producing. A bent piece of card is not a particular efficient wing, but the principle is exactly the same as the lift force that the wings produce in flight.

You might have noticed that no mention has been made of the engine. This is because the production of lift is independent of the power from the engine. The wing of a glider produces lift just as the wing of an airliner does. What the engine does is produce the *thrust* necessary to get the aircraft moving through the air in the first place, and to overcome *drag* once the aircraft is moving.

Thrust opposes drag

Drag is the force which resists the movement of an aircraft (or any other object) through the air. In level flight, thrust must be equal to drag to maintain a constant airspeed. A typical light aircraft might produce 70kg of drag in the cruise, thus requiring the engine to produce 70kg of thrust to maintain a constant airspeed. For the mechanically inclined, a typical training light aircraft engine will have four cylinders with a total capacity of up to 4000cc (i.e. 4 litres) and be capable of producing 100 to 150 horsepower. The engine will turn the propeller relatively slowly (about 2200 Revolutions Per Minute – RPM – being a typical cruise power setting) because the propeller loses efficiency if it is turned at more than about 3000RPM.

During level flight a light aircraft is using thrust to overcome drag and keep the aircraft moving through the air at a constant airspeed. If you take away the engine power, simply allowing the aircraft to descend gently will achieve an airspeed fast enough to produce sufficient lift to keep the aircraft airborne, albeit in a shallow glide. This is not dissimilar to a car 'coasting' down a slope, with gravity providing the forward propulsion. Most light aircraft are surprisingly efficient gliders, and from a height of 2000 feet a typical training aircraft may be able to glide for several miles. Landing without engine power is not particularly difficult in a light aircraft and is the sort of thing practised regularly during training.

Now we have covered the basic principles of flight. As a summary, in straight and level flight at a constant airspeed, the four forces act as shown below:

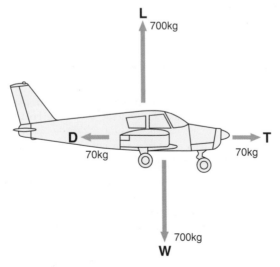

In the Air

In the Air

There is a story about a research team who wanted to record the sensation of somebody making their first parachute jump. They found a volunteer, and spent months training and coaching him to be able to narrate the forces and sensations he was going to experience. Then he was equipped with sophisticated monitoring equipment and wired with a mini voice recorder. After the necessary training the big day came, our hero climbed into the aircraft and it roared off. At the pre-arranged height he stepped out onto the strut and jumped.

Safely back on the ground the researchers gathered round the recording tape in anticipation. It contained just one word: "Yaahhhhhooooo!"

The point of this story is to illustrate that like any new experience, the sensation of getting airborne is a subjective one, sensed differently by different people. The feeling may be one of revelation, a dream fulfilled, possibly a little nervousness, or just mild curiosity.

In a small aircraft you will tend to experience more movement than in a large aircraft, just as a small boat will be more affected by a sea conditions or wind than a large ship. Any movement is unlikely to be excessive, it's just a question of it being a new and unfamiliar sensation. The air tends to become smoother as you climb, and in any case you will probably soon stop noticing this movement as your senses adjust to flight and you become involved in the flying of the aircraft.

If you have been used to flying only as a passenger in airliners, you may be surprised at just how much visibility there is from a light aircraft through the windscreen and canopy or side windows and as you climb higher, prominent landmarks such as mountains, woodland or nearby towns will become visible. You may be able to recognise these, if not the instructor will be pleased to point-out and name the major landmarks around. Remember, don't be afraid to ask questions: most instructors are secretly quite pleased to be able to show off their knowledge! At this early stage of the flight the instructor will be routing away from the airfield and climbing to the cruising altitude. Take the opportunity to orientate yourself and enjoy the view. You may have unintentionally tensed-up during the take-off, if so make a conscious effort now to relax, you will enjoy the flight much more when you do.

A typical view from about 2000 feet

With the aircraft levelled-out and settled in the cruise, the time has come for you to try some flying for yourself.

Firstly, the instructor will demonstrate the effect of the flying controls. Looking ahead, you should be able to see the horizon and the position of the nose of the aircraft in relation to it – this is known as the *attitude*. A normal 'straight and level' attitude may look something like this:

The 'normal' straight and level attitude

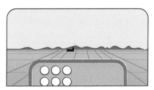

The instructor may now apply some back pressure to the control column. Note the phraseology here: there is no question of pulling the control column hard back: huge and violent control movements are the stuff of badly-made films and TV. The total movement of the control column is unlikely to be anything more than a few centimetres, and if you imagine the input required as a pressure rather than a movement you will be thinking along the right lines. Returning to the demonstration, as the instructor applies some back pressure on the control column, look ahead, and you will see the nose pitching up gently. This pitching will continue as long as the back pressure is held. When the back pressure is released, the aircraft will stop pitching up. At this higher nose attitude the aircraft is likely to be climbing gently at a slower airspeed than when it was flying level, because the aircraft is going uphill. If the horizon has disappeared under the nose you may find it useful to look down the side of the nose to get a better idea of the attitude.

Back pressure on the control column makes the nose pitch-up, and the aircraft will start to climb

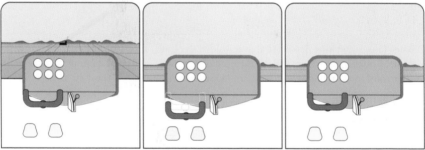

The whole demonstration is much quicker than a written description, and after applying some back pressure the new, higher nose attitude may look something like this:

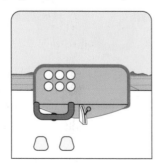

Forward pressure on the control column
makes the nose pitch-down, and the
aircraft will start to descend

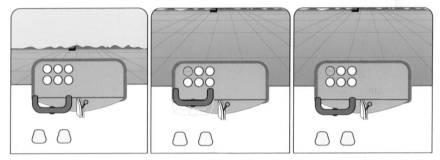

Now to look at pitching down. All that is needed is a gentle forward pressure on the control column. Looking ahead you will see the nose pitch down gently, and continue to do so until the forward pressure is relaxed. At this lower nose attitude the aircraft is likely to be descending gently at a faster airspeed than when it was flying level. The new, lower nose attitude may look something like this:

The instructor may have asked you to place one hand *lightly* on the control column while demonstrating this so that you can get the idea of the relationship between control movement/pressure and change in attitude. Following the demonstration in this way is known, innocently, as 'following through'. Remember to expect to apply a pressure to the control column, rather than making a large movement. Think of the way you would handle the steering wheel of a car travelling at 100mph or more, and treat the control column in the same way. As you try out the flying controls the instructor will talk you through the manoeuvre, prompting the actions needed. In technical terms you have now seen the primary effect of the elevators: forward and backward movement of the control column controls pitch.

Now your instructor will demonstrate the side to side movement of the control column. Looking ahead, when the instructor moves the control column to the right (which means rotating a control wheel to the right), you will see that the aircraft banks to the right – this movement is known as roll. The aircraft will continue to roll for as long as the control

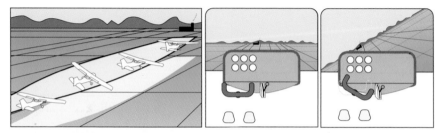

When the control column is moved to the right, the aircraft will now roll to the right

column is held over. When it is returned to neutral the aircraft will stay, more or less, at the new angle of bank and the aircraft will be turning in direction in which it is banked (ie, when banked to the right, the aircraft will turn right). Again the amount of control movement needed is small, but a bit more than the movement used when controlling in pitch. The picture outside may look something like this:

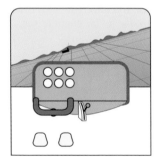

The instructor will return the aircraft to a wings-level attitude, then bank the aircraft to the left by moving the control column to the left. Now you will see the aircraft turning to the left and the picture outside will look a bit like this:

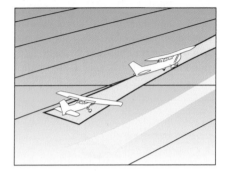

When the control column is moved to the left, the aircraft will roll to the left

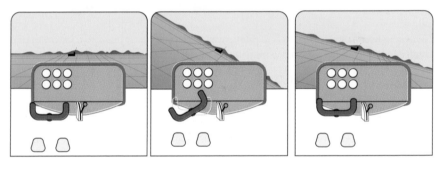

Again, the instructor may invite you to try this for yourself to get a feel for how the aircraft reacts to the control movements. You have now seen the primary effect of the ailerons: moving the control column from side to side controls roll.

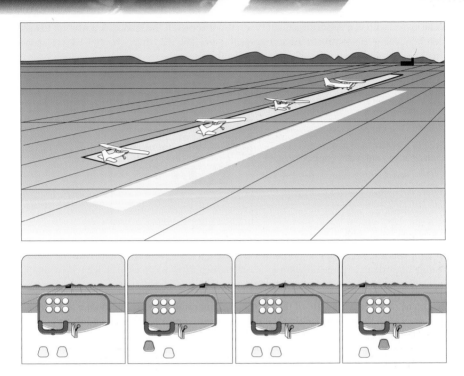

Using the rudder pedals makes the aircraft yaw

The instructor may also demonstrate the use of the rudder. Pressing the right rudder pedal causes the nose to yaw (skid) to the right, and vice versa. However, many instructors choose not to demonstrate the use of the rudder during the introductory lesson, instead they leave the use of the rudder until the next flying lesson of the PPL course (Exercise 4 – Effects of Controls).

Now that you have seen how the control column is used to control the aircraft in pitch and roll, it is time to put this knowledge into practice by flying the aircraft straight and level. To demonstrate this, the instructor will settle the aircraft in straight and level flight, heading towards a prominent landmark.

A constant level is maintained by keeping the nose at the 'level' attitude. If the nose is too high, the aircraft will start to climb; use forward pressure on the control column to return to the desired attitude. If the nose is too low the aircraft will start to descend, use back pressure on the control column until the nose is back at the desired attitude.

The aircraft is kept flying straight by keeping the wings level. For example, if the aircraft is left wing low, move the control column to the right until the wings are level again, then centralise the control column. If the aircraft is right wing low, move the control column to the left until the wings are level again, then centralise the control column. To assess if you are maintaining a constant direction, choose a clear landmark ahead. As long as it stays in the same spot ahead, you are maintaining a constant direction. If the landmark moves off to one side, you will need to bank the aircraft towards it, levelling the wings when it is ahead again.

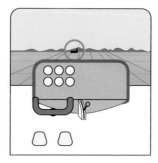

Choose a distant landmark ahead to check that you are maintaining a constant direction

All of this is far simpler to do than to describe. The control movements needed to maintain straight and level flight are as instinctive as driving a car in a straight line, with the added feature of working in three dimensions instead of two. Now you have seen what is required, you will get a chance to put it into practice.

For many people the thought of the instructor relinquishing control to them is a daunting one, even with the knowledge that the instructor sitting next to them has a full set of dual controls. There is no reason to feel vulnerable. Unlike learning to drive, where a movement of just a few feet from a given path can have unfortunate consequences, in the sky there is a lot of space to move around in. This means that the instructor can allow you to get a feel for controlling the aircraft, without having to intervene the moment the aircraft moves away from a precise flight path. In fact, at this stage the instructor will usually only intervene to change direction or level, or if you ask him or her to!

It is worth remembering that in cruising level flight, the aircraft does not require intensive control movements. The instructor may demonstrate that the aircraft will fly quite happily 'hands off', with only minimal intervention from the pilot. With this in mind, you can apply yourself to flying the aircraft.

Within a few minutes you will find that the control of the aircraft, maintaining straight and level flight, is not a complicated task, and soon becomes almost instinctive. That said, there are two common errors often made when first learning to fly, they are:

■ over-controlling, and

■ gripping the controls too hard.

Over-controlling happens when the pilot makes control movements much larger than those actually required, for example pulling back too far on the control column when trying to correct a nose-low attitude. The result is that the aircraft pitches up too far, and you are faced with a nose-high attitude. If you reverse the error (pushing forward too fast or too far) the nose pitches down too far, and you have the beginnings of a roller-coaster ride! You may catch a smile on the face of your instructor, perhaps remembering his or her own first attempt at flying an aircraft. Over controlling like this is not a comfortable way to fly around. If over-controlling happens to you, simply take a deep breath, relax, and let go of the control column (yes, let go). The aircraft will settle back towards the required attitude

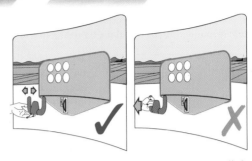

(possibly with some subtle assistance by the instructor) and then you can try again, with a conscious effort to make the control movements smaller, slower and smoother. Incidentally, the oscillations caused by over-controlling are known to pilots as Pilot Induced Oscillation – PIO. This is one of those useful aviation phrases to remember for later if you want to impress your friends with the story of your flight - "There was a little PIO, but I soon sorted that out..."

Gripping the controls too hard can be a cause of over-controlling and will also make it more difficult for you to sense the pressures and movements needed on the control column. Look down at your hand; if it is gripping the control column as if your life depends on it (probably with the knuckles starting to show white), then you are holding the control column far too tightly. Again the solution is simple: take a deep breath, relax your grip, and try again. To avoid over-controlling try placing just your thumb and two fingers on the control column. This way it is more difficult to grip the control column too tightly, and you will be able to feel the movements of the controls far more easily.

Because on this flight you will be staying fairly close to the airfield, you cannot fly too far in a straight line and so your instructor may encourage you to make some of the turns yourself. To turn, simply bank the aircraft in the direction you want to turn in, centralising the control column when you have a reasonable angle of bank. The aircraft will start to turn in the direction that the aircraft is banked to. As the aircraft is turning, apply a little bit of back pressure on the control column, as the nose tends to pitch down slightly during a turn. When you want to stop the turn, choose a new landmark as an aiming point and simply level the wings again, remembering to anticipate by starting to 'roll out' of the turn just before the new landmark is directly ahead.

Later in the lesson, the instructor may also give you the chance to alter the power setting (for example, reducing the power to start a descent). The throttle (the equivalent of a car accelerator) will be of a 'quadrant' type or a 'plunger' type. These work as illustrated below:

If power is reduced, the aircraft will tend to pitch down. If you allow the aircraft to take up a lower nose attitude, it will start a gentle descent.

When flying straight, the HI will read a constant heading

Once you feel that it is becoming easier to fly the aircraft, you may want to look at some of the instruments. The Airspeed Indicator (ASI) will show the aircraft's speed through the air, a figure of 100knots/110mph is typical for a training aircraft, maybe 20mph slower for a three-axis microlight. Of course, at altitude there is little sensation of speed because there is nothing nearby to act as a reference. Nevertheless, if you are flying over an area you know well, you will realise how quickly the aircraft covers the distance between points that are many road miles apart. The Heading Indicator and compass shows the direction of the aircraft in degrees. When flying straight, the heading should remain constant. The altimeter will indicate the aircraft's altitude. When flying level the altitude should remain constant.

When flying level the altimeter will show a constant level. This altimeter is reading 2000ft

Although you may want to look at the instruments for interest, do not try to fly the aircraft by sole reference to them, it is far more difficult than it looks. Even if you do manage to get one instrument, say the Heading Indicator, to read exactly as you want it; you can guarantee that some other parameter, for example the altitude, will now be going wrong. Controlling the aircraft by reference to the view outside is by far the best way to learn how to fly at this stage. Deviations of up to 20°-30° in heading and 200-300 feet in altitude are not usually a problem in an introductory lesson and besides, looking outside gives you a chance to enjoy the view too.

You'll find the aircraft easier to fly if you concentrate mostly on the view outside

Whilst concentrating on flying the aircraft, you will probably notice little else and the time will pass very quickly. If you do feel at all unwell, tell your instructor so that he or she can help. As a general rule the act of flying the aircraft prevents queasiness, and looking ahead rather than moving your head around a lot may also help. The instructor will be able to open fresh air vents if you want. Above all, don't worry. The sensation of flying in a light aircraft can take a little getting used to, but any queasiness will soon pass.

A typical 'General Aviation' airfield (in the case Caernarfon, in Wales), seen from 2000 feet

WIND

Correct allowance made for drift

All too soon you will find yourself returning to the airfield, and descending prior to landing. At some stage the instructor will take over the flying again, but (s)he will keep you informed of what is happening as you near the airfield. As you descend the effect of any wind may become more noticeable again. This is particularly so if there is a crosswind at the landing runway. A crosswind is the situation when the wind is blowing at an angle across the runway in use. An aircraft cannot disregard the effect of wind on its flight path, if there is a crosswind the pilot has to make allowance for it during the final approach to land. This is usually done by heading the aircraft slightly into wind to counter the drifting effect caused by the wind. This may mean that although the aircraft is tracking directly towards the runway, the nose is actually pointed to one side of the runway. The visual effect can be a bit disconcerting to the uninitiated, looking to one side to see the runway. Nevertheless, it is a perfectly normal procedure for landing in crosswind and is the sort of thing you will practice as part of the PPL course.

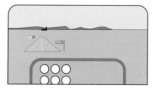

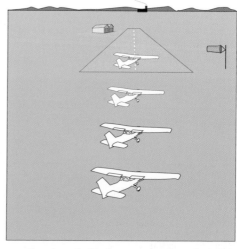

If you have not watched a landing from the cockpit before this may be one of the highlights of the flight. The pilot will level-out the aircraft just a few feet above the runway and begin to pitch the aircraft gently nose up aiming to land gently on the mainwheels, making a series of control movements until the aircraft touches down. Once on the ground, gentle braking and steering will follow as the instructor slows the aircraft to turn off the runway. All-in-all the whole procedure is probably far more gentle and smooth than landing in an airliner, with no noisy reverse thrust or harsh braking. Most pilots get great satisfaction from a good landing, and if the touchdown has been particularly smooth you may see a smile of satisfaction on the face of your instructor.

The view of the runway from a light aircraft on final approach

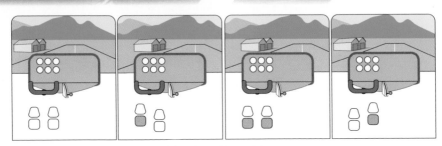

Steering the aircraft on the ground using the rudder pedals

Having vacated the runway and completed the after-landing checks, the aircraft is taxyed back to the parking spot. The instructor may offer you the chance to steer the aircraft with the rudder pedals, depending on conditions. Beware, directional control on the ground can seem quite strange after flying the aircraft, don't be surprised if your first attempts at taxying seem very hard work!

Back at the parking spot the instructor will apply the parking brake and then shut down the engine. You may find the silence quite startling after getting used to the noise of the airflow, the engine and the radio chatter All there is now is the sound of the instrument gyros running down and the occasional 'pinking' noise as the engine cools; your first flying lesson is over.

What Now?

What Now?

Back in the flying school the instructor will need to complete some paperwork formalities, and there may be an introductory lesson certificate waiting for you. The flying school staff will probably ask you if you enjoyed the flight, and ask if you want to take flying any further. This might be a difficult question and you may want to know a bit more about the course and the licence itself.

The Private Pilot's Licence

The introductory lesson is the first flying lesson of the course for the Private Pilot's Licence (PPL). Before looking at the training course, it makes sense to know about more about the PPL itself.

The PPL can be likened to a driving licence. It is the basic qualification that can be the goal in itself, or the first step to a career in flying. The PPL entitles you to fly single-engine aircraft in daylight and in reasonable weather conditions. There are two types of light aircraft PPL available in the UK – the EASA/JAR-PPL and NPPL. Each has slightly different requirements and privileges which are described shortly. There is also a PPL specifically for flying microlight aircraft, also described shortly.

Once you have completed the PPL course, you do not have to buy your own aircraft – indeed the vast majority of PPLs do not have their own aircraft. You will be able to hire an aircraft from the flying school you learnt with, who will probably also have more advanced touring aircraft that you can move up to. There are several hundred flying organisations in the UK alone where you can hire everything from a simple training aircraft or microlight such as the one you learnt on, up to exotic aerobatic and vintage aircraft and long-distance touring machines.

To use the PPL there are two main requirements:

Medical – you must have a current medical certificate or medical declaration (described shortly)

Currency – you must fly a minimum number of hours in a defined period – typically 12 hours in 12 months – and make one flight every two years with an instructor.

Clearly these requirements are not onerous, and most pilots fly more than the legal minimum.

As already stated, most pilots do not own their own aircraft, but you should not think that it is exorbitantly expensive to do so. If you just want to get airborne, and are not too worried about taking passengers with you, a single seat aircraft or microlight can be purchased for well under £10,000. As you might expect, here is virtually no top limit to what you can spend on an aircraft.

Rather than owning an aircraft yourself, an alternative is to join a group, where a number of pilots all share the ownership of an aircraft. The practicalities of belonging to an aircraft group are outside the scope of this book, but it is a very popular way to have the use of an aircraft whilst sharing the costs amongst several people.

There are several thousand airfields throughout Europe, so you should never be short of places to visit. There are also several hundred flying events each year in the UK alone. These vary from the informal 'fly-in' at a small airstrip where you can literally drop in for a chat, to much larger or more organised events such as major air displays where visitors by air are spared the traffic jams before and after the show. There are also many air rallies, usually with mini-competitions such as spot landing, navigation, etc.

Air shows, rallys and fly-ins are a great opportunity to meet fellow pilots

For many pilots, the PPL itself is just the start of a long flying career. Many pilots go on to expand their skill and experience by qualifying to fly more complex types than the training aircraft they learnt on, for example aircraft with turbo-charged engines or retractable undercarriage. You may choose to fly multi-engine (ME) aircraft and obtain other ratings to fly at night, in cloud, or to fly aerobatics.

Pilots can fly around the UK and abroad, and the PPL can be validated in many other countries with minimal formalities. More exotic aircraft, such as seaplanes, tail wheel, kit-built, vintage or even or some ex-military jets, can be flown by PPL holders who have completed the necessary conversion training.

In reality, the basic PPL allows a pilot to take flying as far as he or she wants, to coin a cliché, the sky really is the limit!

You might move to multi-engine aircraft

Pre-Entry Requirements

There are no formal pre-entry requirements for starting the PPL course. You should be basically literate and numerate, but there is nothing in the course or written exams that will disadvantage anybody with basic educational qualifications. There is no minimum age for learning to fly, although you cannot obtain a PPL until you are 17. At the other end of the scale there is no maximum age for learning to fly or holding a PPL, there are several pilots in the UK alone who have learnt in their 70s and are still active in their 80s. Before flying solo you must obtain a medical certificate (EASA/JAR-PPL) or medical declaration (NPPL and microlight PPL), more details are given in the appendix.

You can only fly as Pilot In Command (e.g. without an instructor or qualified pilot) if you have a valid medical. If you have any queries about the medical and its requirements it is a good idea to contact the CAA's Medical Division at an early stage.

An instrument flying qualification allows you to fly in more difficult weather conditions

An aerobatic rating opens up a new kind of flying

The PPL Course

The flying time of an introductory lesson counts towards the flying hour requirements of the Private Pilot's Licence course. The PPL course itself consists of a minimum number of flying hours (currently 45 for a EASA/JAR-PPL, 32 for a NPPL), together with a certain amount of studying to pass multi-choice examinations on subjects such as Air Law, Meteorology, Navigation, Human Factors, Principles of Flight etc. The Microlight PPL involves less hours (25 hours, or 15 for a licence with 'operational limitations') and slightly different written examinations. This is largely a reflection of the fact that a microlight is a simpler machine than an average light aircraft, and more restricted in its performance and operating limitations. For all types of flying licence, the 'minimum' flying hours are just that – you should expect to need more than the absolute minimum to reach the required standard.

You should realise at the outset that you do not have to sign up for a full course in order to start learning to fly and for a light aircraft there is also no requirement to commit to the choice between a EASA/JAR-PPL or NPPL until well advanced along the PPL course. You can book lessons as often (or as rarely) as you like, and you can pay for each lesson as you take it. Until the cross-country navigation stage of the course is reached, an average flying lesson will last about 1 hour. There is no time limit for completing the course, although someone who can commit to a full-time course can probably complete it in around four weeks. For those who are flying in their spare time, anything from 9 to 18 months is closer to average. Ideally you should try to take your lessons every 2 weeks or so (or more frequently if you can), especially in the early stages. If your lessons are too far apart you may find that you have to spend time in the air just revising previous exercises before you can progress. Bear in mind too that the weather plays an important role, especially in the early stages of the course. Flying in bad weather is a waste of your time and money and no instructor will do this if the weather makes it likely that you cannot properly complete the lesson.

Simply starting flying lessons in no way obliges you to complete the course. Many people start with the aim of simply seeing how things progress, or perhaps aiming for the first solo, and there is nothing wrong with that. Many flying schools offer various schemes of block-booking and pre-payment which reduce the cost of lessons and these can be worth considering.

Aside from the flying itself, the school may offer evening or weekend lectures for the examination subjects, which are integrated with the flying syllabus. You will need certain training materials as you progress – a logbook, maps, text books, navigational equipment etc. The school can advise you what you need and when to buy it, and most flying schools carry a stock of this equipment. Many schools also have a reasonably active social scene, and even when you are not flying you will find many pilots and trainees around. Happily there are also many good airfield cafes to eat and watch the airfield activity, even on a day when you are not flying.

After the introductory lesson, the next flying lesson is Exercise Four (the Effects of Controls), which explores in more detail not just the main flying controls you will have used in the introductory lesson, but the ancillary controls too. You will then progress through more straight and level flying, climbing, descending, turning and flight at slow airspeeds. This will lead you into the 'circuit', where you will practice take-offs and landings. Then comes the moment when your instructor steps out of the aircraft and sends you off for your first solo flight. This is truly a never-to-be-forgotten moment; even veteran pilots with a lifetime of flying behind them will be able to tell you when and where they made their first ever solo flight.

More circuit flying follows, practising different take-off and landing techniques, interspersed with more solo flying. This leads to map reading and navigation flying, and ultimately you will make the 'qualifying cross country' flight – a solo flight in which you fly away from the home airfield to land at other airfields before returning to base.

At the end of the course, and after some revision, you will take some form of 'Skill Test'. This is a flight with an examiner which consists principally of flying the manoeuvres and demonstrating the techniques that you have learnt throughout the course.

With the 'Skill Test' passed, the school will assemble a small pile of paperwork relating to your training course and exams, help you fill-out the relevant forms, and then the whole lot disappears into the post. In return you will get the coveted piece of paper - your PPL - that opens-up the world of flying to you.

Some of the text books available for the PPL course

Pilot's Logbook Record

Pilot's Logbook

Airplan Flight Equipment

www.afeonline.com

| Medical Expires | / / | | Class/Type Rating Expires | / / |

YEAR	AIRCRAFT			Holder's Operating Capacity	FLIGHT DETAILS		Depart Time	Arrival Time	DAY			DAY		NIGHT		Remarks
Date	Type	Registration	Captain		From	To			Single-Engine (SE)			T-O LDG		T-O LDG		
									In Command	Dual or P2						

I certify that the entries in this log are true

Pilot's Signature _____

Abbreviations and Glossary

Abbreviations and Glossary

AOPA	The Aircraft Owners and Pilots Association
Apron	The part of the airfield where the aircraft are normally parked
ASI	Airspeed Indicator
ATC	Air Traffic Control
AVGAS	AViation GASoline – the fuel used by most light aircraft
BMAA	British Microlight Aircraft Association
Book-out	The process of notifying ATC or the airfield operator of the proposed flight
CAA	The Civil Aviation Authority, responsible for regulating flying in the UK
Canopy	The glass area over the cockpit
Carb.	Carburettor
CFI	Chief Flying Instructor
Circuit	The traffic pattern around the airfield for aircraft arriving and departing
Coaming	The shelf or ledge on top of the instrument panel
CPL	Commercial Pilot's Licence
Crosswind	A wind blowing at an angle across the runway or the flight path of the aircraft
EASA	European Aviation Safety Agency
Final	The approach to land, when the aircraft is lined up with the runway and descending towards it
HI	Heading Indicator
Holding Point	A point where an aircraft stops before entering or crossing the runway. This is usually where the power and pre take-off checks are completed
IAS	Indicated Air Speed
JAR	Joint Aviation Requirements
Knot	One nautical mile per hour, a speed of 10 knots is 10 nautical miles per hour.
Mph	Miles per hour
NPPL	National PPL
PIC	Pilot In Command – during the introductory lesson the instructor is the PIC
PPL	Private Pilot's Licence
PTT	Press To Transmit, the radio transmit button
QFE	The pressure setting on the altimeter sub-scale which allows the altimeter to read height above the airfield
QNH	The pressure setting on the altimeter sub-scale which allows the altimeter to read altitude above sea level
Tech. log	Technical log, forms and logbooks individual to an aircraft in which all its flights are recorded
Threshold	The beginning of the runway, where the runway numbers may be painted

The Phonetic Alphabet

The Phonetic Alphabet

The 'phonetic' alphabet, in which each letter is given a name and specific pronunciation, is used extensively in aviation, not just on the radio. The table below gives the phonetic word and pronunciation for each letter:

Letter	Phonetic Word	Pronunciation
A	Alpha	**AL** FAH
B	Bravo	**BRAH VOH**
C	Charlie	**CHAR** LEE
D	Delta	**DELL** TAH
E	Echo	**ECK** OH
F	Foxtrot	**FOKS** TROT
G	Golf	GOLF
H	Hotel	HOH **TELL**
I	India	**IN** DEE AH
J	Juliett	**JEW** LEE **ETT**
K	Kilo	**KEY** LOH
L	Lima	**LEE** MAH
M	Mike	MIKE
N	November	NO **VEM** BER
O	Oscar	**OSS** CAH
P	Papa	PAH **PAH**
Q	Quebec	KEH **BECK**
R	Romeo	**ROW** ME OH
S	Sierra	SEE **AIR** RAH
T	Tango	**TANG** GO
U	Uniform	**YOU** NEE FORM
V	Victor	**VIK** TAH
W	Whiskey	**WISS** KEY
X	X-ray	**ECKS** RAY
Y	Yankee	**YANG** KEE
Z	Zulu	**ZOO** LOO

Useful Addresses and Contacts

Useful Address and Contacts

AFE

Airplan Flight Equipment
1a Ringway Trading Estate
Shadowmoss Road
Manchester
M22 5LH
Tel: 0161 499 0023
www.afeonline.com

AOPA

Aircraft Owners and Pilots
Association
50a Cambridge Street
London
SW1H 4QQ
Tel: 020 7834 5631
www.aopa.co.uk

BMAA

British Microlight Aircraft
Association
Bullring
Deddington
Oxon
OX15 0TT
Tel: 01869 338888
www.bmaa.org

CAA

Civil Aviation Authority
CAA House
45-59 Kingsway
London
Tel: 020 7379 7311
www.caa.co.uk

Magazines:
Flight Training News
www.flighttrainingnews.co.uk
Flyer Magazine
www.flyer.co.uk
Microlight Flying
www.bmaa.org
Pilot Magazine
www.pilotweb.co.uk
Todays Pilot Magazine
www.todayspilot .co.uk

JAR PPL
and NPPL
Differences

JAR PPL and NPPL Differences

At the time of writing, most UK flying schools (other than microlight schools) offer the choice of a EASA/JAR-PPL or NPPL. In principal the EASA/JAR-PPL involves a longer course of training, leading to a licence with greater privileges and to which further ratings and qualifications can be added. The medical standard for the EASA/JAR-PPL is more stringent and the revalidation requirements slightly more involved than for NPPL. The NPPL offers a quicker route to a PPL, with less stringent medical standards, for those who are prepared to accept reduced licence privileges compared to EASA/JAR-PPL. The NPPL can be 'upgraded' to an EASA/JAR-PPL by completing a minimum of a further 15 hours of flying training.

The EASA/JAR-PPL is issued after a course of flying training (minimum 45 hours) completed in accordance with Joint Aviation Requirements (JAR), with licence syllabus and privileges harmonised across most European States. Therefore an EASA/JAR PPL is valid in most European countries and indeed, with some paperwork formalities, it is accepted virtually worldwide. To hold an EASA/JAR-PPL it is necessary to hold at least a valid JAR class 2 medical certificate. This medical certificate can only be issued by an Authorised Medical Examiner (AME – a doctor qualified to issue aviation medicals).

The National PPL (NPPL) is issued after a course of flying training (minimum 32 hours) completed in accordance with the NPPL syllabus, which is specific to the UK The NPPL is not accepted outside the UK and additional ratings and qualifications cannot be added to it. To hold a NPPL (or a microlight PPL) it is necessary to hold at least a valid medical deceleration, equivalent to DVLA Group 2 standard, which can obtained from your own doctor or GP.

Medical Validity

Age	JAR Class 2	DVLA Group 2
Under 30	5 years	Unlimited
30-44	2 years	Unlimited
45-49	2 years	5 years
50-65	1 year	5 years
65 and over	1 year	1 year

Comparison table:

	JAR PPL	NPPL
Minimum Course Hours	45 hours	32 hours
Medical Standard	JAR Class 2	DVLA Group 2
Licensed to fly outside UK	Yes	No
Additional ratings available (e.g. night, instrument, multi engine)	Yes	No
Licence validity	5 years	Unlimited
Class rating on initial licence issue	Single Engine Piston (SEP) aeroplane	Simple single engine aeroplane
Class rating validity	24 months	24 months
Instructional flight required to maintain licence validity	Yes, 1 hour every 24 months	Yes, 1 hour every 24 months
Limitation on number of passengers	No	Yes – three maximum
Minimum hours to maintain validity	12 within the 12 months before rating expiry	6 within the 12 months before a flight

Definitions:

Simple Single Engine Aeroplane:

A single engine piston aeroplane with a maximum take-off weight authorised (MTWA) not exceeding 2,000kgs (but not a microlight or a self launching motor glider).

Single Engine Piston (SEP) Aeroplane:

A land-based aeroplane powered by a single piston engine.

Microlight:

An aeroplane with a maximum total weight authorised (MTWA) not exceeding 450 kilograms for two seat aircraft and 300 kilograms for single seat (for a landplane) and a stalling speed at maximum total weight authorised not exceeding 35 knots.

To fly light aircraft with different features or handling characteristics to those of the training aircraft used for the PPL course, certain 'differences training' must be completed.

Differences training required:

Feature	JAR PPL	NPPL
Tricycle (nose wheel) undercarriage	No	Yes
Tail wheel	Yes	Yes
Supercharged or turbocharged engine	Yes	Yes
Variable pitch propeller	Yes	Yes
Retractable landing gear	Yes	Yes
Cabin pressurisation	Yes	Yes
Maximum continuous cruising speed in excess of 140 knots IAS	No	Yes

Index

Index